CRUSH • LOVE POEMS

Also by **Kwame Alexander**

Poetry

Dancing Naked on the Floor: Poems and Essays
Kupenda: Love Poems
360°: A Revolution of Black Poets (ed.)
Just Us: Poems and Counterpoems

Non-Fiction

Do The Write Thing: 7 Steps to Publishing Success
Tough Love: The Life and Death of Tupac Shakur (ed.)

Fiction

The Way I Walk: Stories and Poems for Young Adults (ed.)

CRUSH • LOVE POEMS

KWAME ALEXANDER

Published by Word of Mouth Books
www.mycrushbook.com
Copyright © 2007 by Kwame Alexander
Introduction Copyright © 2007 by Christine Compo-Martin
Additional Copyright information listed on page 69

ISBN: 978-1888018-40-0
LCCN: 2007922663

Book Design: Sagetopia, LLC
Editor: Christine Compo-Martin

CRUSH is available wholesale from Small Press Distribution, Baker & Taylor, or
directly from the Publisher. For educational discounts and classroom examination
copies, contact Stephanie Stanley at Stephanie@bookinaday.com

10 9 8 7 6 5 4 3 2
Printed in the U.S.A.

To

students and teachers everywhere, especially
Oscar Smith High School,
The Nora School,
& Crossland High School,
I thank you for your appreciation and inspiration;
but most of all, I celebrate your imagination

and

the lady in the library,
Kathy Allen
thanks for sharing the love
(and the great food).
"Holy smokes, we did it KA!"

THE AUTHOR WOULD LIKE TO EXPRESS...

Sincere Thanks

Dianne Beverly, Marshall Johnson, Donna Maria Smith, Karyn Langhorne, Laura Bruce, Joanna Crowell, Mike Williams, Deanna Nikaido, Stacey Evans Morgan, Tinesha Davis, Maritri, VINX, Shana Tucker, Karla Scott, Sue Grisewood, Kim Hardwick, Carol Varsalona, Eva Jones, Rich Dooner, Nikki Giovanni, E. Ethelbert Miller, Cleve Francis, Larry Butti, Jim Smith, Phyllis Schirle, Stan Bustetter, Dr. Janet Andrejco, Shana Yarborough, Marita Golden, Michael D. Harrison, Marjorie Light, Kate Messner, Gabrielle Faulcon, and Dana Davidson.

Special Thanks

The Alexanders and Stanleys (especially Ndali Brume, Jayla Stanley, and Mekhi Hewling), Tanya Hill, Yvette Willis, Kathy Allen, Christine Compo-Martin, and Janell Walden Agyeman of Marie Brown & Associates (A genuine writer's advocate).

Extraordinary Gratitude

my creative muse, Nandi; and my forever crush, Samaraca. Kupenda!

CONTENTS

III. Crushed

INTRODUCTION

When I first heard Kwame sing-out his visions, I was hooked. Looking around the packed room, I could see I was not alone. As one, we bobbed with his rhythms, rode the swell of his vibrato, wiped tears from our eyes as his truths melted our collective hearts. As one, we stood and signaled our connection. He beamed. We radiated. In our stolen moments of together we gave testimony to his mission. *A poet.*

Like the dusty circuit preacher of yesteryear, Kwame has traveled cross-country to recruit soldiers of the heart, rebellious wordsmiths, and determined dreamers to his cause. In every school and every library, he has danced before teachers and students alike, conjuring *meaning* out of ink, pulling truth out of thin sheets of paper, calling *cool* down from the heavens and wrapping it in ribbons of *intense.*

"Poetry is alive, it speaks to you...It is the blood running through your veins that keeps you laughing and loving." His voice coaxes, lures, jolts and shocks complacency out of the atmosphere and banishes it to the oily corners of the boiler room. *"Poetry is magical."*

And so *Crush: Love Poems* is born.

Inside these pages are poems that transform, transcend, and transport. Whether you're living through the oh-so-consuming teenage days now...or delving into the dusty memory box hastily shoved under the bed...here are poems that are *so cool...*

Poems that vibrate off the page. Poems that paint the *first* love, the *last* love, the *never will again* love, the *don't know what it even is* love.

Poems that sometimes whisper, sometimes shout, but always sing. Poems that snort and chuckle. Poems that lick their lips and smile. Poems that triumphantly raise the trophy of a shiny new love and place it prominently on the mantle of our memory.

He wishes he were a library, each
book she would check out.

Father, son, sage, unrequited lover, born-to-be lover, singer, dancing dreamer and determined believer...Kwame the poet is *Cool...so cool.*

Christine Compo-Martin
Brasher Falls, New York

I. Memoirs of First Love

Eventually, They'll Jump In

He watches
Her read
The way her fingers
Delicately turn each page
At times
He wishes
He were a library
Each book she would check out

She listens
To his voice
The way it soars through the air
Defying space and time
For a moment
She wants to be his lips
Have him feel her name
Over and over again

They sit
In silence
Their thoughts like
Crashing waves
Eventually
They feel the ocean's pull
Each hoping the other
Will take a swim

A Lover's Concerto or The Fine Art of Flirting

Think of me
        as your own
Private Symphony
My hair the piano keys your fingers dance on
My lips the oboe your tender mouth sings through
My arms the tambourines that vibrate with your touch
My hips the bass drum tense from your glance
My legs two piccolo trumpets blazing through the air

Yes, think of me
        as your own
Private Symphony
And perhaps one of these days,
When water is free, and heat is complimentary
When sex is safe and shoes don't cost so much
When perms are permanent and love is forever
You know, the way things are supposed to be
Perhaps one day
I might let you
Strum my cello

Haiku

u and i shun love
two unnamed stars in sacred
space   afraid to shine

Standing in the Checkout Line, Reading *In Touch* Magazine, Emily Jackson Has Decided What She Wants

is a kind of real love.
the end-of-a-movie *predictable* love
the Duracell battery *everlasting* love
the rock-paper-scissors *playful* love
the Italian marble *unbreakable* love
the "made in America" *dependable* love
the Ancient Egypt *sophisticated* love.
the Krispy Kreme *way too sweet* love
And, if you can give her
what she needs,
in return,
she'll give you some
of that Super Wal-Mart kind of love
(not the everyday low price kind of love)
You know,

*That **24/7, Always Open** kind of love*

Tanka

your laughter is a
joyful noise that sings to me
like a Baptist choir
on first Sunday, so strong
it makes me wanna *holla*

I Want You

        to think of me   as
Ellington thought of jazz and
Ella thought of scat   as
Lady Day thought of loss and
Luther thought of love

yes, think of me
as the first aria and
the last allegro
in this symphony
of life

in other words
let this ancient language of love
be the music
that keeps you
humming through the night

that keeps you
dancing
naked
on the
floor

"Your Blues Ain't Like Mine," he thinks

In the middle of the Civil War
right after Lee's Battle at Appomattox
and before Lincoln freed the slaves

Somewhere between the stale
pizza and Robert Frost
physics and the drama club meeting

I joined the ranks of a million guys
who've planned as much as an army general
rehearsed more than a Broadway play

Before asking you out
before being told
"I'll think about it"

Beneath the Summer Moon

you catwalk past me like
some sun-wrapped angel

on a Parisian nightcloud.
it's those legs,

so long, so deep,
they simply flow

like The River Seine
sous la lune d'été

Love Poem #1

I've got you under my skin
An ocean floor
A buried treasure
This is not a want
I need you
Like book needs page
Like winter needs snow
Like my lonesome heart
Needs the red stream of life
I've got you deep in the heart of me
So deep in my heart,
that you're really a part of me
I guess this is a start
a hot spring poem
wrapped in me
for you to wear outside
when the rain comes
and the sea fills
Yes, I've got you under my skin

What Makes Me Feel Good

       isn't
the way you style your hair or
how all the other girls stare
it's not even the way you kneel
in church, unafraid of prayer

       it's
this fire we share
the gentle way you care
our friendship is like a common cold
i declare
       you are the fever
       that burns in this affair

Love Poem #9

i want
our first time
to be
the last leaf of Fall
the first Winter snowflake
a purple orchid that blooms in Spring
two peach-faced lovebirds learning to fly
under the Summer moon

II. Kupenda: The Remix

The Examination

(AKA The *Before-You-Holla* Quiz)

Can you study my heart, and learn to love me with your mind?

Can you lift my spirits, bench press my burdens, exercise my intellect?

Can you get deep like Atlantis, precise like Google, outstanding like a Serena Williams serve?

Can you love me like a book of poetry, read me over and over, uncover the magic between my lines?

Can you solve me like a quadratic equation, recite Neruda in Spanish? Forget sexy, can you bring *SmartBack?*

Can you flirt with me like an E. Ethelbert Miller poem, tease me like a Bossa Nova song?

Can you sweet-talk me with cotton candy on a rainy day, love me like Nikki Giovanni loves Tupac?

Can you speak to me with your mouth closed?

Can you kiss me 100 times with your eyes open?

Can you love me...with your mind?

Kupenda

lips like yours
ought to be
worshipped

praised
called to the altar
dipped in water and wine

see, i ain't never been
too religious
but you can baptize me

anytime.

Haiku

if i am your heart
imagine me inside
beating, pumping, loving

He Says He Loves Me

        and tells me not to worry
That he has protection.
I ask him does he have enough of it
To guard my heart
To give shelter to my soul
        in case of emergency.

Awkward Poems

Sometimes I wish we weren't friends
then i could gaze into your bold eyes
and find answers to questions i'm afraid to ask
but for now, i'll stick to quick glances
and other friendly gestures

Sometimes i wish we weren't friends
then i could hold your hands in ways
that made your palms moist from suggestion
but for now, i'll stick to high fives
and other friendly gestures

Sometimes i wish we weren't friends
then i could hijack your bronze lips,
take them hostage and steal their suppleness
but for now, i'll stick to light pecks
and other friendly gestures

What i am trying to say is
I love
glancing
lingering
flirting
and being your friend

but one day
one day real soon
i'm gonna put away those
big
soft
dark
friendly gestures
and get close
get real close to you

but for now, i'll stick to awkward poems
and other friendly gestures

The Girl from Puerto Rico

Show me a little piece of heaven
Tómeme a sus fronteras esponjosas

Amid the white sandy beaches
En el pico del fuego

Remember me to Boqueron
Donde ángeles cantan

Where beauty abounds
Y el amor se jubila

Southern Love Song

I know my honey cares for me
> See, I asked her for a dollar
> and she gave me three
Now I've dated a lot of girls in my life,
> 'but you, one day, gonna be my wife'

I know my sugar's love is true
> See, I told my momma
> and she told hers too
Now I've dated a lot of girls in my life,
> 'but you, one day, gonna be my wife'

I know my baby's heart is mine
> See, she tells me all the time
> I'm fine
Now I've dated a lot of girls in my life,
> 'but you, one day, gonna be my wife'

My girl's been asking how I feel
> Wants to know
> are my feelings real
So I proceed to kiss her on her lips
> Politely place my hands on her hips

Whisper these words in her ear
       And hope she doesn't get too excited
       to hear
That I've dated a lot of girls in my life,
       'but you, one day, gonna be my wife'

Haiku

quiero subir
su montaña, inhalar
y nade nubes

Kupenda

I have never committed a crime
Yet I want to steal your tongue

I have never been arrested
Yet my mouth is in your custody

I have never gone to jail
Yet your lips imprison me

If I were a poet in love
I'd say that with you

I have found that new place
Where the only thing that matters

Is the newfound freedom
From a cool calm kiss

Haiku

being alone is
a nightmarish journey
barefoot on Everest

Spellbound

"When I go to high schools the thing I tell the young men is you start writing poetry and you will always win. Write poems and learn how to slow dance" —Sherman Alexie

without u
i am lost

as in: isolated
unfinished   broken off

shipwrecked on the shore of solitude
ankle deep in possibility

i have read the dictionary
twice

and still there r no words
to fill my blank spaces

to punctuate the way i feel
when yr smile two-steps

across the stucco walls
of my memory

perhaps
i will open a thesaurus now

and find a little piece of hope
or something similar

III. Crushed

Letting Go

When   you read this
Poem   forget about the
Words   consider the space between
Them   a reminder of my life without
You

Love Poem #101

You said our relationship
was sorta like school,
that I was failing your class,
and should study harder.
Well, maybe I need a better teacher.

Current Affairs

I don't know much about the laws that govern subway trains
or local policy, but during breakfast my mother watches the news,
and there is talk about some new transportation legislation that will
expand the routes to benefit commuters who live farther out. I care
as much about this as I do about golf, which is why my Dad is not
here. Okay, maybe less. I wash the dishes, by hand, my mother's
way of teaching me how to be self-sufficient. After college, first
thing I will buy with my first check: *A Maytag Jetclean III*. Believe
that! Sleep beckons me, which I know is a peculiar way to say
'I'm tired,' but we're reading Shakespeare in English, and he
'beckons' a lot. I am off to school, a one-hour and ten minute ride
on the train, where I will either study for my Biology test, or nap.
Guess which one I do. I am heading to Addison Road, the final
stop on the Blue line. The woman next to me fidgets a little and
wakes me up. Damn her! I glance at her, ready to growl, or at least
think mean thoughts, until I see him. Braids, White Teeth (that's
important), A slight scar, No earring (Thank goodness, cuz that's
so cliché), Muscles, Faded jeans, black 21's, and a jersey—with no
undershirt—of some basketball player (Did I mention muscles?).
He is fine, and I am staring very hard. Then he looks at me, and
I almost fall down, only I am sitting. I quickly pull out a book to
read, some memoir about somebody, somewhere, who had a rough
childhood. Maybe I should write a book. The lady next to me is a
religious woman, judging from the worn out King James Bible she

is fixated on (not to mention her baseball cap that reads: *Jesus is Coming, Look Busy!*) Alrighty then! The train comes to a sudden halt, like some kid pulled the emergency break, jolting us forward. This sends King James into the aisle, where several commuters accidentally step on it and kick it. This, of course, sends Church Lady into a frantic fit. She fusses and cusses, left and right, back and front—in the name of The Lord. Before I can laugh at her, the hot boy from across the aisle finds his way through the madness, scoops up King James (like he just stole the ball in a game of one-on-one), and presents it to Church Lady—like it's her fortune, or something. She's quiet now, watching this gift from God (My gift, her God). He bends down, on one knee, as if in half-prayer, and I notice his tattoo. Church Lady takes the Bible from his dark, strong hands—so strong they could smash granite—and offers a smile. And a thank you kiss, on his cheek. What! She pulls him even closer, and I am not the least bit worried that I am gawking. This cannot be happening. She whispers something in his ear, he smiles—there's that pearly smile that beckons my soul—and kisses the scar on his right cheek. He lights up, not like a flicker, but a flame. My phone rings, and I'd rather not answer, as I am captivated by the three words inked on his neck: *I Miss You.* I flip my *Motorola RAZr* open, and Dad says, "What's the meaning of life, baby girl?" the same thing he's been saying to me every morning since I can remember. Hello is not in his vocabulary. "Heaven, Dad, it's all about a little piece of sky," I answer, and for the first time I think I know what it means. *What have I missed?*

Dad wishes me a great day from the golf course, the train makes its final stop, and he vanishes like the stars at dawn. *Now, I am awake.* I just wish I had more time. With him. We are both two trains running. And in this moment I decide that I will take an interest in current affairs, and learn to play golf. Sunday school's a possibility too.

Why I Hate Astronomy

My date with Claudia
lasted exactly 6.2 hours:
>   the length of time
>   it took Venus
>   to cross the Sun's disk
>   before she vanished from sight.
See?

Michelle

and i were tight, once,
like windows painted shut
in a world
where stares and shock
are as common as reality TV
and race is a four-letter word for
"I don't understand you, and I won't try"

We found in each other
A Bliss whose color was gray
            Like the confederate uniform her Father wore
            At weekend reenactments
A Freedom whose history we rewrote
            each day we embraced
A Laughter as loud
            as a nuclear roar
but it turns out the joke was on us
because in an instant
our future exploded

We were tight
until I punked out
gave in to my fears
of a world

where everything
is black and white
of a life
where mixed feelings
are a no-win situation
and love loses every time

In My Closet, On The Top Shelf, Is A Silver Box

Journal, filled

Candy bar, unwrapped

Picture, Kevin

Flower, Kevin

Poems, Kevin

Library card, mine

Naomi Shihab's *What Have You Lost?*, overdue

Saturday, late

Us, movies

Laughing, loving

Later, strolling

Me, "I want chocolate"

Kevin, "You already sweet enough, baby"

Store, closing

We, hurrying

Colliding, customer

Accident, sorry

Guy, angry

Me, craving

Kevin, Hershey

We, pay

Turn, leave

Surprise, a rose,

Pink, favorite

Me, "thanks"

Outside, "Hey!"

Guy, earlier

Kevin, ignore

Hands, holding

Walking, fast

Giant, steps

Me, turn

Guy, points

aims, fires

rips, back

Kevin, drops

candy, sidewalk

Rose, falls

Guy, runs

Blood, runs

Kevin, "you alright?"

Me, "Kevin!"

Eyes, closing

Me, "I Love You"

Kevin, "More than a Kit Kat?"

We, laugh

Sirens, scream

Heart, pierced

Love, bleeds

Hope, dies
Hands, empty
Sweetness of life, gone
What, remains
picture, Kevin
flower, Kevin
candy bar, unopened
locked, away
inside, silver box
top shelf, in my closet

High School Blues Suite (in Five Parts)

She was my first crush
Breaking up never crossed my mind...
If you see me laughing
I'm laughing to keep from crying...

I. Used

after three hours
together
she left
with my heart
in one hand
and my homework
in the other

II. Conversation After Lunch

"it's not that i don't
love you," she says. "indeed,
i want to kiss you...

"...to lasso your lips
tame them, ride them, rein them in
to my stable, but

"first, my love, you must agree
to commit...to a breath mint"

III. Haiku

i am overwhelmed
with gloom. my sweet love gone like
ashes over bridge

IV. Note Found in My Locker

don't haiku me
anymore
i want an epic
that i can trust
to be around
for more than
a moment

V. Crushed

We lost. The night is not so beautiful
anymore. I can no longer see the stars.
Maybe they are tired and miserable, like me, or
They simply refuse to come out anymore, like you.
I miss you. I thought I could will us to win,
by praying, and wanting, and...hoping, but,
not tonight. My defense was lousy. I can't
stop thinking about what happened.
I am in a quandary. So was the coach.
He didn't want to lose...again, either. I
still hear the sound of the buzzer...ringing.
Why haven't you called? The sound of losing
is disappointing, a test I've failed to study for.
I want to know why? I was the star, finally
Unafraid to shine, remember? We had a near perfect
record, remember? And I was always willing to practice.
But, nothing can prepare one for this
kind of defeat. Being cut is one thing.
Finding you in the opposing team's
locker room is another.

This game is over.

Plus...
5 Poems by Poets Mentioned in Crush

Communication

If music is the most universal language
Just think of me as one whole note

If science has the most perfect language
Picture me as mc^2

Since mathematics can speak to the infinite
Imagine me as 1 to the first power

What I mean is   one day
I'm gonna grab your love
And you'll be
Satisfied

-Nikki Giovanni

I Would Steal Horses

For Kari

for you, if there were any left,
give a dozen of the best
to your father, the auto mechanic
in the small town where you were born

and where he will die sometime by dark.
I am afraid of his hands, which have
rebuilt more of the small parts
of this world than I ever will.

I would sign treaties for you, take
every promise as the last lie, the last
point after which we both refuse the exact.

I would wrap us both in old blankets
hold every disease tight against our skin.

—*Sherman Alexie*

Toothpaste

After dinner
You have the habit
Of curling up in
The couch
Like a tube of
Toothpaste all bent
Funny and nice
I like to brush
After every meal

—*E. Ethelbert Miller*

Tonight I Can Write (excerpt)

Tonight I can write the saddest lines.

Write, for example, 'The night is starry
and the stars are blue and shiver in the distance.'

The night wind revolves in the sky and sings.

Tonight I can write the saddest lines.
I loved her, and sometimes she loved me too.

Through nights like this one I held her in my arms.
I kissed her again and again under the endless sky.

She loved me, sometimes I loved her too.
How could one not have loved her great still eyes.

Tonight I can write the saddest lines.
To think that I do not have her. To feel that I have lost her.

To hear the immense night, still more immense without her.
And the verse falls to the soul like dew to the pasture.

What does it matter that my love could not keep her.
The night is starry and she is not with me.

—*Pablo Neruda, translated by W.S. Merwin*

Crush

A girl wrote a letter on an orange
And placed it on a doorstep.

That day the sky tasted fresh as mint.

—*Naomi Shihab Nye*

ABOUT KWAME ALEXANDER

KA has written eight books, owned several publishing companies, written for the stage and television, recorded a CD, performed around the world, produced jazz and book festivals, hosted a weekly radio show, worked for the U.S. Government, and taught in a high school...But, what he loves to do most, is watch his teenage daughter become a smart and beautiful woman, listen to his brilliant and wonderful wife laugh, and sit in his library reading and writing poems about both of them.

> Kwame Alexander's poems are suffused with honesty, humor, beauty, and a sometimes raw authenticity that makes them compelling to young adults and mature readers.
> —*Dana Davidson, author of Played and Jason & Kyra*

> "His poetry is unforgettable...truly lovely and larger than life."
> —*3BlackChicks.com*

> "Inspiring...entertaining...fresh."
> —*Press-Republican*

For more information on KA, or to have him present at your school, library, conference or event, contact Stephanie@bookinaday.com or visit *www.KwameAlexander.com*

CRUSH CONTEST

Tell us about the love in your life. That's right,
in 30 lines or less, write a poem (haiku, free
verse, sonnet, etc.) about dating, breaking up,
best friends, or what crush means to you.

Regular winners will have their poems posted at www.mycrushbook.com and
one lucky Grand Prize winner will win a jazz and poetry concert at your school,
featuring Kwame Alexander and his band.

For official rules and entry forms go to *www.mycrushbook.com*

Word of Mouth Books

Get your copy of Crush today at your local bookstore, online at *amazon.com*,
or *www.mycrushbook.com*